Wood Pellet Smoker Cookbook

The Best Recipes Included to Smoke and Grill Meat, Fish, Game, and Etc.

Chad Davis

TABLE OF CONTENTS

INTRODUCTION 7

Wood Pellet Smoker Use Tips 9

Food safety 9

Wood Pellet Smoker Tips 10

Smoking And Grilling Tips 11

Chapter 1/ Beef 12

Swirling Smoked Tournedos 12

Zesty Filet Mignon 14

Nutty Clod Steak 17

Smoke From The Porterhouse 19

Soot On The Flanks 22

Chapter 2/ Pork 24

Sauce in The Pork Belly 24

Asian Ribs 27

The fate of The Front Hock 29

Steak with Me 32

Peppery Pork Tenderloin 34

Chapter 3/ Lamb 36

On Chop of The World 36

The Cold Shoulder 39

Smoldered Lamb Shank 41

Chocolate Lamb 44

Chapter 4/ Poultry 46

Zesty Smoked Chicken Breasts 46

Smoked Wings on Sesame Street 48

Chicken, Smoked and Tender 50

Juicy Turkey Breast fillet 52

Juicy Breast Steaks 55

Chapter 5/ Fish 58

Tuna Burgers 58

Savory Smoked Sardine 60

Please Sir, Can I Have Salmon? 63

Smoke at The Bay 66

Shrimps on Fire 68

Chapter 6/ Vegetables 70

Smoked Potatoes with Honey 70

Rad Radish 73

Smoked Butternut Squash 76

Chapter 7/ Game 78

Rabbit in The Grill Light 78

Go and Venison No More 80

Smoked Duck Legs 83

CONCLUSION 86

INTRODUCTION

Smoking is known for being one of the most well-known cooking methods nowadays. And these smoked foods, in general, are rich in protein and healthy fats that could be spoiled or can lose its rich flavours with inappropriate, modern cooking techniques. And on this framework, we offer you this Wood Pellet Smoker and Grill cookbook that will just be your perfect cooking slow cooking guide to the smoking cooking method that you can use to cook any type of meat. Indeed, the idea of smoking food and meat itself is an exciting idea that brings up the taste of spring and summer to your dish and that

encourages you to cook whether indoors or outdoors. For instance, smoking is a low cooking process of meat with which you can preserve the flavour or your food and at the same time, it will make it even more flavourful. Smoking meat is more than simply cooking; it is more an art than a simple cooking method. And with the Wood Pellet Smoker and Grill, you don't have to be a professional cook to use it; all that you need to do is to read this cooking guide and you will find out how with a little practice and time, even though you might have never used a Wood Pellet Smoker and Grill, you will excel in using it. And once you become an expert with using the smoking technique, you will never look for any other cooking methods and techniques. All you have to do is to download the Wood Pellet Smoker and Grill and learn some basic techniques and you are just there. So, if you want to learn about the smoke cooking technique; you have come to the right place and you have chosen the most suitable cookbook that will guide you through your smoke cooking journey. This Wood Pellet Smoker and Grill cooker offers you not only a large and mesmerizing array of gourmet dishes, but it also teaches you healthier ways to prepare food and meats in particular. And what is more special about Wood Pellet Smoker and Grills is that this cookbook makes you desire your food more and it uses less harmful substances from. Therefore, we can say that this Wood Pellet Cooker does not only please the eye with the inviting look of dishes we can cook with this technique, but this device is versatile. Furthermore, Wood Pellet Smokers and Grills can be fuelled with various types of wood pellets; each with a specific flavour. Besides, Wood pellet Smoker and Grills can perfectly fit into our busy days and schedules and we can use it on a daily basis. However, in flipping through the wide variety of recipes and dishes; you will be able to learn how to marinate different types of meat and blends for several hours and you will be able to cook large cuts of meat without having to worry if it will burn. In this book, you will find delicious recipes that vary from seafood to different types of poultry and meat and you can familiarize yourself with mouth-watering recipes to get the very best dishes from steaks to fish, seafood, pork and poultry dishes. And you will be surprised that with a Wood Pellet Smoker and Grill; you can roast, braise and even bake whatever dish you want. So what are you waiting for to fire up your Wood Pellet Smoker and Grill and get ready to enjoy one of the most unique culinary experiences that you can ever enjoy and try.

Wood Pellet Smoker Use Tips

Using a Wood Pellet Smoker and Grill can be very easy if you follow the following tips and safeguards:

Food safety

Make sure to keep everything clean in the kitchen and make sure to maintain the cooking area clean as well. You can use different utensils and platters for the cooked meat in the kitchen than the one you used to use with the raw meat. And this will prevent any type of contamination of any type of bacteria.

The marinade or the basting sauce should have its own tools and utensils.

Wood Pellet smoker and grill may help you keep foods warm and can keep cold foods cold as well.

You should never save a marinade to use it later at a later time and if you are going to serve it with the meat; you have to make sure to let it boil.

Cooked foods shouldn't be left out in the heat for a period that exceeds an hour. So try not to leave hot foods out of refrigeration more than two hours.

Marinade and defrost any type of meats through refrigeration. Do never try to thaw meat at a room temperature or on top of a counter. Bacteria can grow quickly in moist and warm foods; so make sure to wash your hands with soapy and hot water before starting any meal preparation whether it is made of fish, fresh meat or poultry.

Wood Pellet Smoker Tips

Whenever you want to switch from high temperature to low temperature; make sure to lift the lid and leave it open until the actual temperature becomes close to the desired temperature you are looking for. And this can speed up the process and can ensure that the fire won't go out.

Always be prepared when you prepare your recipes with the right accessories, utensils and all the grill sides that you will need when you start cooking. You should also read the entire recipe from starting it to the end.

Using a BBQ floor mat may be very useful, especially due to different food handling accidents. So, using a cooking spatter and a BBQ floor mat can protect. You can use a stone platform too.

SMOKING AND GRILLING TIPS

To infuse more flavours and smoke into any meat you choose to cook, you should cook it for a longer time and at a low temperature. Cook for a longer time and at a low temperature. The meat will close after the fibres after it reaches about 120°F. Mopping and misting; are also great ways to keep your meat from dying out.

While searing the meats, cook with the lid down and always make sure to use a meat thermometer to determine the internal temperature of the foods you choose to cook.

Remember that smoking foods with the hardwood pellets will turn your poultry and meats pink.

Sugar-based sauces are also best applied when the cooking process is about to end up.

Always leave the space open between foods and extremities of the barrel for a proper heat flow. Crowding food require more cooking time.

Make sure to use a set of long-handled tongs to turn meats in addition to a spatula for turning fish and burgers. With a piercing utensil; like a fork, you can prick the meat before letting it rest.

Foods in deep casseroles usually require more time to cook in comparison to shallow baking pans.

It is also a good idea to place the cooked food on a heated platter in order to keep your food warm.

Red meats like beef roast and steak should be set aside for several minutes to rest before serving it and this allows the juices to add more flavour.

Chapter 1/ Beef

Swirling Smoked Tournedos

TOTAL COOK TIME 45 MINUTES

Ingredients for 2 servings

The Beef

- 2 tournedos (0.5 lb.)

The Rub

- Salt – ¼ teaspoon
- Almond butter – 1 teaspoon
- Hazelnut extract – ¼ teaspoon
- Garlic powder – ½ teaspoon
- Basil powder – 1 teaspoon
- Chili powder – ½ teaspoon
- Cloves powder – ½ teaspoon
- Canola oil – 1 teaspoon

The Smoke

- Preheat the smoker at least 1 hour before smoking.
- Use oak wood pellets for smoking.

Method

1. Combine the salt, almond butter, garlic powder, hazelnut extract, basil powder, chili powder, cloves powder, and canola oil in a bowl. Mix thoroughly.
2. Rub the spices mixture on each tournedos thoroughly. Allow the tournedos to stand for 50 minutes.
3. Prepare your grill by cleaning the grates. Add oak wood to the grill and light it at least 1 hour before you start grilling.
4. When the grill reaches 180°F, place the tournedos on the grate. Grill each side for 15 minutes.
5. Remove the tournedos from the grill and allow to stand for 15 minutes.
6. Cut then serve.

Zesty Filet Mignon

TOTAL COOK TIME 5 HOURS

Ingredients for 4 servings

The Beef

- 1 filet mignon (1 lb.)

The Marinade

- Apple Cider Vinegar – ¼ cup
- Salt – ½ teaspoon
- Garlic powder – 1 teaspoon
- Onion powder – 1 teaspoon
- Chili powder – ½ teaspoon
- Dill weed powder – ¼ teaspoon
- Sage powder – ¼ teaspoon

The Smoke

- Preheat the smoker at least 30 minutes before smoking.
- Use hickory wood pellets for smoking.

METHOD

1. Combine the salt, garlic powder, onion powder, chili powder, dill weed powder, and sage powder in a bowl. Mix thoroughly and set aside.
2. Place the filet mignon in a bowl and add apple cider vinegar to the bowl. Cover the bowl and allow the filet mignon to marinate for 5 hours.
3. After 5 hours, drain the marinade from filet mignon. Add spices mixture to the filet mignon and rub generously. Cover seasoned filet mignon and place it in the fridge overnight (8 hours).
4. When the seasoned filet mignon is ready, remove it from the refrigerator and allow it to thaw.
5. Prepare your grill, clean the grates. Then add hickory wood to the grill and light it at least 30 minutes before smoking.
6. When the grill reaches 200°F, place the filet mignon on it and grill for 4 hours. Occasionally turn the sides while it grills.
7. Remove from the grill and allow to stand for 20 – 30 minutes.
8. Cut then serve.

NUTTY CLOD STEAK

TOTAL COOK TIME 6 HOURS 40 MINUTES

INGREDIENTS FOR 4 SERVINGS

THE BEEF

- Clod steak (1 lb.)

THE RUB

- Salt – ½ teaspoon
- Peanut powder – 1 teaspoon
- Allspice – 1 teaspoon
- Garlic powder – ½ teaspoon
- Basil powder – 1 teaspoon
- Chili powder – 1 teaspoon
- Cloves powder – ½ teaspoon
- Almond butter – 2 teaspoons
- Canola oil – 1 teaspoon

THE SMOKE

- Preheat the smoker at least 1 hour before smoking.
- Use oak wood pellets for smoking.

METHOD

1. Combine the salt, butter, and spices in a bowl. Mix thoroughly.
2. Cut the clod steak into 2 thin halves.
3. Rub the spices mixture on each half of the clod steak thoroughly. Place the seasoned steaks in a refrigerator for 12 hours.
4. Prepare your grill by cleaning the grates. Add oak wood to the grill and light it at least 1 hour before you start grilling.
5. When the grill's temperature reaches 250°F, place the clod steaks on the grate. Grill for 6 hours while turning the sides every 1 hour.
6. Remove the clod steaks from the grill and wrap in 2 layers of foil paper for 30 minutes.
7. Unwrap, cut then serve.

Smoke From The Porterhouse

TOTAL COOK TIME 55 MINUTES

Ingredients for 5 servings

The Beef

- 1 porterhouse (1.5 lb.)

The Rub

- Salt – ½ teaspoon
- Onion powder – 1 teaspoon
- Garlic powder – ½ teaspoon
- Basil powder – 1 teaspoon
- Chili powder – 1 ½ teaspoon
- Cloves powder – ½ teaspoon

The Garnish

- Peanut powder – 1 tablespoon

The Smoke

- Preheat the smoker at least 30 minutes before smoking.
- Use pecan wood pellets for smoking.

METHOD

1. Combine the salt and spices in a bowl. Mix thoroughly.
2. Rub the spices mixture on the porterhouse thoroughly. Allow the porterhouse to stand for 3 hours.
3. Prepare your grill by cleaning the grates and removing the ashes. Add pecan wood to the grill and light it at least 30 minutes before you start grilling.
4. When the grill reaches 200°F, place the porterhouse on the grate. Grill each side for 15 minutes.
5. Remove the porterhouse from the grill, wrap in food-safe butcher paper, and allow to stand for 20 minutes.
6. Cut, drizzle peanut powder over the cutlets then serve.

Soot On The Flanks

TOTAL COOK TIME 1 HOUR 5 MINUTES

Ingredients for 8 servings

The Beef

- 1 flank steak (2 lbs.)

The Rub

- Salt – ½ teaspoon
- Onion powder – 1 teaspoon
- Ginger powder – ½ teaspoon
- Garlic powder – ½ teaspoon
- Thyme – ½ teaspoon
- Chili powder – 1 teaspoon

The Garnish

- Pineapple juice – ¾ cup

The Smoke

- Preheat the smoker at least 30 minutes before smoking.
- Use hickory wood pellets for smoking.

Method

1. Combine the salt and spices in a bowl. Mix thoroughly.
2. Rub the spices mixture on the flank steak generously. Allow the flank steak to stand for 1 hour 30 minutes.
3. Prepare your grill by dusting, cleaning the grates, and removing the ashes. Add hickory wood to the grill and light it at least 30 minutes before you start grilling.
4. When the grill reaches 180°F, place the flank steak on the grate. Grill each side for 20 minutes.
5. Remove the flank steak from the grill. Place in a saucepan, add the pineapple juice and cover for 15 minutes.
6. Drain the pineapple juice from the flank steak.
7. Cut then serve.

Chapter 2/ Pork

Sauce in The Pork Belly

TOTAL COOK TIME 5 HOURS 10 MINUTES

Ingredients for 6 servings

The Pork

- Pork belly (1.5 lbs.)

The Rub

- Salt – ¾ teaspoon
- Onion powder – 1 teaspoon
- Ginger powder – ½ teaspoon
- Garlic powder – 1 teaspoon
- Almond nut powder – 1 teaspoon
- Cayenne powder – 1 teaspoon
- Cinnamon powder – ¼ teaspoon

The Sauce

- Tomato sauce – 1 cup

The Smoke

- Preheat the smoker at least 45 minutes before smoking.
- Use apple wood pellets for smoking.

METHOD

1. Trim off any fat layer on the pork belly.
2. Combine the salt and spices in a bowl. Mix thoroughly.
3. Rub the spices mixture on the trimmed pork belly generously. Allow the pork belly to stand for 2 hours.
4. Clean your grill in preparation for grilling. Add applewood to the grill and light it at least 45 minutes before you start grilling.
5. When the grill reaches 220°F, place the pork belly on the grate. Grill each side for 1 hour.
6. Remove the pork belly from the grill and place in a saucepan.
7. Add tomato sauce and mix well until both sides of the pork belly are covered with the sauce.
8. Allow the sauced pork belly to stand for 40 minutes. Light the grill while the pork belly stands.
9. Place the sauced pork belly back on the grate. Grill each side for 1 hour or until the internal temperature is 170°F.
10. Remove from the grill and let it stand for 15 minutes.
11. Cut then serve.

Asian Ribs

TOTAL COOK TIME 10 HOURS 15 MINUTES

Ingredients for 4 Servings

The Meat

- 24 country-style pork ribs

The Marinade

- Soy sauce – 2 cups
- Fresh ginger, grated – 4 tablespoons
- Sherry – 2 cups
- 6 cloves of garlic, peeled and crushed

The Smoke

- Preheat your smoker to 220° F
- Hickory wood pellets are recommended for this recipe

Method

1. In large-size bowl, combine the marinade ingredients (soy sauce, sherry, ginger and garlic).
2. Add the ribs to the marinade and turn the ribs over to evenly and well coat. Cover and chill in the fridge overnight.
3. In a single layer, arrange the ribs directly on the preheated smoker rack and smoke for between 2-3 hours. The internal temperature on a meat thermometer should register 160° F
4. Serve with your favorite dip.

THE FATE OF THE FRONT HOCK

TOTAL COOK TIME 3 HOURS 30 MINUTES

Ingredients for 4 servings

The Pork

- 1 Front hock (1 lb.)

The Marinade

- Chicken broth – 2 cups
- Lime juice – 1 cup

The Rub

- Salt – ¼ teaspoon
- Garlic powder – ½ teaspoon
- Basil powder – 1 teaspoon
- Red pepper flakes – 1 teaspoon
- Cinnamon powder – ½ teaspoon
- Olive oil – ½ teaspoon

The Smoke

- Preheat the smoker at least 1 hour before smoking.
- Use apple wood pellets for smoking.

METHOD

1. Combine chicken broth and lime juice. Soak the front hock in this mixture for 24 hours.
2. Combine the salt, spices, and olive oil in a bowl. Mix thoroughly.
3. Rub the spices-oil mixture on the marinated front hock thoroughly. Allow the front hock to stand for 30 minutes.
4. Clean the grates of the grill and remove old ashes. Add applewood to the grill and light it at least 1 hour before you start grilling.
5. When the grill reaches 200°F, place the front hock on the grate. Grill each side for 90 minutes or until the internal temperature is 160°F.
6. Remove the hock from the grill, wrap in food-safe butcher paper and allow to stand for 20 minutes.
7. Unwrap the front hock, cut then serve.

STEAK WITH ME

TOTAL COOK TIME 45 MINUTES

INGREDIENTS FOR 4 SERVINGS

THE PORK

- 2 pork steaks (0.5 lb.)

The Rub

- Salt – ½ teaspoon
- Peanut powder – 1 teaspoon
- Allspice – 1 teaspoon
- Garlic powder – ½ teaspoon
- Onion powder – 1 teaspoon
- Chili powder – 1 teaspoon
- Caramel sauce – ½ cup

The Smoke

- Preheat the smoker at least 30 minutes before smoking.
- Use maple pellets wood for smoking.

Method

1. Combine the salt, caramel sauce, and spices in a bowl. Mix thoroughly.
2. Rub the spices mixture on each pork steak thoroughly. Let the seasoned pork steaks stand for 1 hour 15 minutes.
3. Prepare your grill. Add maple wood to the grill and light it at least 30 minutes before you start grilling.
4. When the grill's temperature reaches 220°F, place the pork steaks on the grate. Grill each side for 13 minutes.
5. Remove the pork steaks from the grill and wrap them in 1 layer of foil paper for 10 minutes.
6. Unwrap, cut each steak into 2, then serve.

Peppery Pork Tenderloin

TOTAL COOK TIME 3 HOURS 40 MINUTES

Ingredients for 10 servings

The Pork

- 1 pork tenderloin (1.5 lb.)

The Marinade

- Salt – ½ teaspoon
- Curry powder – ¼ teaspoon
- Onion powder – 1 teaspoon
- Garlic powder – ½ teaspoon
- Red pepper flakes – 2 teaspoons
- Cayenne powder – 1 teaspoon
- Coconut vinegar – 2 cups
- Water – ½ cup

The Smoke

- Preheat the smoker at least 1 hour before smoking.
- Use pecan pellets wood for smoking.

Method

1. Combine the salt and spices in a bowl. Mix thoroughly then add coconut vinegar and water. Stir well.
2. Place the pork tenderloin in the marinade for 18 hours.
3. Remove the tenderloin from the marinade and allow it to drain slightly.
4. Clean the grates and remove the ashes in the grill. Add pecan wood to the grill and light it at least 1 hour before grilling starts.
5. When the grill reaches 225°F, place the tenderloin on the grate. Grill each side for 90 minutes or until the internal temperature is 175°F.
6. Remove the tenderloin from the grill, and let it stand for 30 minutes.
7. Cut then serve.

Chapter 3/ Lamb

On Chop of The World

TOTAL COOK TIME 40 MINUTES

INGREDIENTS FOR 2 SERVINGS

THE LAMB

- 4 lamb chops (0.25 lb. each)

THE RUB

- Salt – 1 teaspoon
- Allspice – 1 teaspoon
- Garlic powder – ½ teaspoon
- Onion powder – ½ teaspoon
- Cardamom powder – 1 teaspoon
- Chili powder – 1 teaspoon

THE GARNISH

- Peanut powder – 4 teaspoons
- Parsley (chopped) – ½ cup
- Tomatoes – 2 berries thinly sliced

THE SMOKE

- Preheat the smoker at least 15 minutes before smoking.
- Use apple wood pellets for smoking.

METHOD

1. Combine the ingredients for the rub in a bowl. Mix thoroughly.
2. Season the lamb chops with the rub. Place seasoned lamb chops in the refrigerator for 6 hours.
3. After 6 hours, remove the chops, and let it thaw.
4. Prepare your grill by cleaning the grates and removing ashes. Add applewood to the grill and light it at least 15 minutes before you start grilling.
5. When the grill's temperature reaches 300°F, place the lamb chops on the grate. Grill for 16 minutes while turning the sides every 4 minutes.
6. Remove the lamb chops from the grill, season with peanut powder, then let it stand for 20 minutes.
7. Cut, garnish with parsley and tomato, then serve.

THE COLD SHOULDER

TOTAL COOK TIME 1 HOUR 50 MINUTES

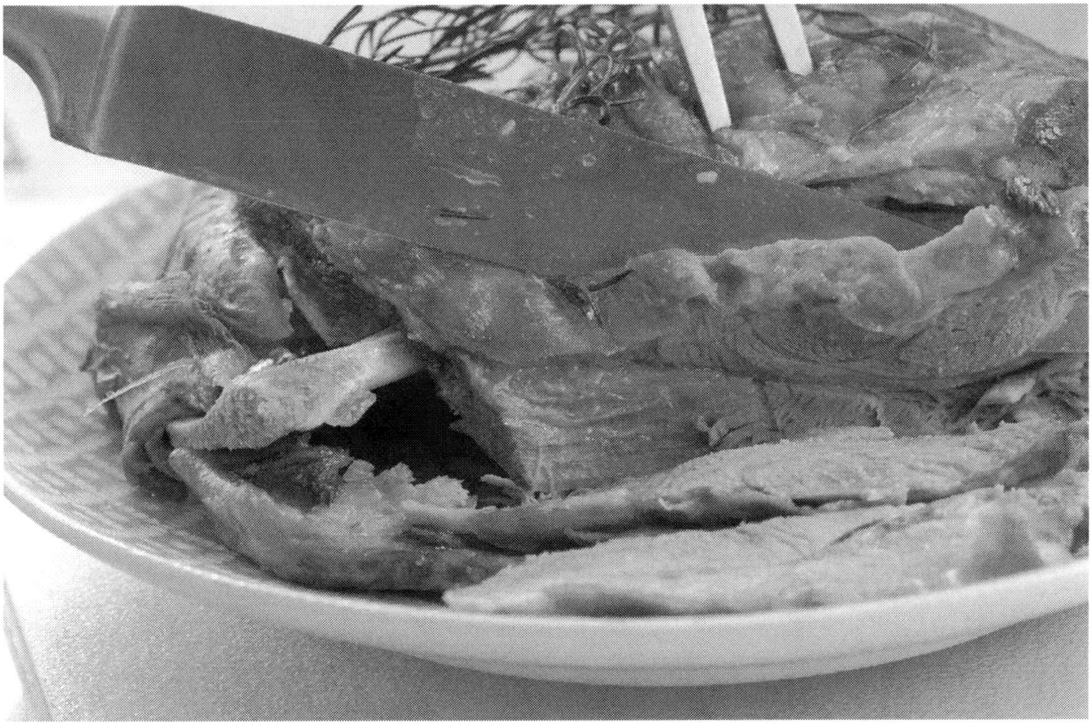

INGREDIENTS FOR 8 SERVINGS

THE LAMB

- 1 lamb shoulder (2 lbs.)

THE MARINADE

- Malt vinegar – 1 cup
- Salt – 1 ½ teaspoon
- Garlic powder – 1 teaspoon
- Onion powder – 2 teaspoons
- Red pepper flakes – 2 teaspoons
- Tamarind powder – ¼ teaspoon
- Sage powder – ¼ teaspoon

THE SMOKE

- Preheat the smoker at least 1 hour before smoking.
- Use mesquite pellets wood for smoking.

METHOD

1. Combine the marinade ingredients in a bowl. Mix thoroughly then set aside.
2. Place the lamb shoulder in the marinade. Cover the bowl and marinate the shoulder for 6 hours.
3. After 5 hours, drain the marinade from the lamb shoulder.
4. Prepare your grill, clean the grates. Then add mesquite wood to the grill and light it at least 1 hour before smoking.
5. When the grill reaches 330°F, place the lamb shoulder on the grate. Grill for 80 minutes or until internal temperature reaches 140°F. Turn every 10 minutes while grilling.
6. Remove from the grill and allow it to stand for 10 – 20 minutes.
7. Cut then serve.

Smoldered Lamb Shank

TOTAL COOK TIME 2 HOURS 30 MINUTES

Ingredients for 2 servings

The Lamb

- 2 lamb shanks (0.5 lb.)

The Rub

- Salt – ¼ teaspoon
- Onion powder – 1 teaspoon
- Garlic powder – ½ teaspoon
- Cloves powder – ½ teaspoon
- Paprika – 1 teaspoon

The Second Rub

- Almond butter – 2 tablespoons

The Smoke

- Preheat the smoker at least 1 hour before smoking.
- Use hickory wood pellets for smoking.

METHOD

1. Combine the ingredients of the rub in a bowl. Mix thoroughly.
2. Rub the spices mixture on each lamb shank thoroughly. Allow the shanks to stand for 4 hours.
3. Prepare your grill by cleaning the grates. Add hickory wood to the grill and light it at least 1 hour before you start grilling.
4. When the grill reaches 300°F, place the shanks on the grate. Grill each side for 15 minutes.
5. Remove the shanks and place them in a saucepan. Add almond butter and stir until the shanks are covered in butter.
6. Place the shanks back on the grate. Grill each side for 45 minutes or until internal temperature is 130°F.
7. Remove the shanks from the grill, wrap in food-safe butcher paper, and let it stand for 15 minutes.
8. Cut then serve.

CHOCOLATE LAMB

(TOTAL COOK TIME 1 HOUR 30 MINUTES)

INGREDIENTS FOR 4 SERVINGS

THE MEAT

- 1 rack of lamb

The Rub

- 2½ garlic cloves, peeled and minced
- Fresh parsley, minced – 1 tablespoon
- Fresh chocolate mint leaves, minced – 2 tablespoons
- Juice and zest of 1 lemon
- Olive oil – 2 tablespoons
- Black pepper – ½ teaspoon

The Grill

- Preheat the wood pellet grill to 300°F with the lid closed

Method

1. In a bowl, combine the olive oil, garlic, lemon juice, lemon zest, chocolate mint parsley, and black pepper to form a paste.
2. Slather the paste evenly over the lamb rack, reserve any excess paste.
3. Place the lamb on the grill and cook until it reaches an internal temperature of 130°F (
4. Take the lamb off the grill and transfer to a serving platter, cover loosely with aluminum foil.
5. Set your grill to open flame, and using tongs, sear the lamb over the flame until it reaches an internal temperature of 145°F

Chapter 4/ Poultry

Zesty Smoked Chicken Breasts

TOTAL COOK TIME 35 MINUTES

Ingredients for 4 servings

The Chicken

- Boneless chicken breast (1 lb.)

The Marinade

- Malt Vinegar – 1 cup
- Salt – ¾ teaspoon
- Garlic powder – 1 teaspoon
- Onion powder – 1 teaspoon
- Cayenne pepper powder – 2 teaspoons
- Thyme – ¼ teaspoon
- Cumin – ¼ teaspoon

The Smoke

- Preheat the smoker at least 1 hour before smoking.
- Use pecan wood pellets for smoking.

Method

1. Combine the ingredients for the marinade in a bowl. Mix thoroughly and set aside.
2. Place the boneless chicken breast in the bowl. Cover the bowl and let the chicken marinate for 3 hours.
3. After 3 hours, drain the chicken.
4. Prepare your grill, dust it, clean the grates, and remove the ashes. Then add pecan wood to the grill. Light the grill at least 1 hour before smoking.
5. When the grill reaches 350°F, place the chicken on it, and grill each side for 10 minutes or until the internal temperature is 160°F.
6. Remove from the grill and allow to stand for 10 minutes.
7. Cut then serve.

Smoked Wings on Sesame Street

TOTAL COOK TIME 33 MINUTES

Ingredients for 4 servings

The Chicken

- 4 chicken wings (1 lb.)

The Rub

- Salt – ½ teaspoon
- Sesame seeds – 1 teaspoon
- Vanilla extract – ¼ teaspoon
- Garlic powder – ½ teaspoon
- Onion powder – 1 teaspoon
- Cumin – ½ teaspoon
- Cloves powder – ½ teaspoon
- Sunflower oil – 1 teaspoon

The Smoke

- Preheat the smoker at least 1 hour before smoking.
- Use cherry wood pellets for smoking.

Method

1. Combine the salt, spices, vanilla extract, and sunflower oil in a bowl. Mix thoroughly.
2. Rub the spices mixture on each chicken wing thoroughly. Allow the wings to stand for 1 hour 30 minutes.
3. Prepare your grill by cleaning the grates. Add cherry wood to the grill and preheat. Ensure you light the grill at least 1 hour before you start grilling.
4. When the grill reaches 350°F, place the wings on the grate. Grill each side of the wings for 8 minutes.
5. Remove the wings from the grill and let them stand for 10 minutes.
6. Cut then serve.

Chicken, Smoked and Tender

TOTAL COOK TIME 36 MINUTES

Ingredients for 2 servings

The Chicken

- Chicken tender (0.5 lb.)

The Rub

- Salt – ½ teaspoon
- Peanut powder – 1 teaspoon
- Allspice – 1 teaspoon
- Garlic powder – ½ teaspoon
- Cloves powder – ½ teaspoon
- Sesame oil – ½ teaspoon

The Garnish

- Peanut crumbs – 2 tablespoons

The Smoke

- Preheat the smoker at least 1 hour before smoking.
- Use pecan wood pellets for smoking.

Method

1. Combine the salt, oil, and spices in a bowl. Mix thoroughly.
2. Season the chicken tender with the mixture and let it stand for 2 hours.
3. Prepare your grill by cleaning the grates. Add pecan wood to the grill and light it at least 1 hour before you start grilling.
4. When the grill's temperature reaches 380°F, place the chicken on the grate. Grill each side for 8 minutes.
5. Remove the chicken tender from the grill. Mix the chicken with peanut crumbs then wrap in 2 layers of foil paper for 15 minutes.
6. Unwrap, cut then serve.

Juicy Turkey Breast fillet

TOTAL COOK TIME 2 HOURS 50 MINUTES

Ingredients for 5 servings

The Turkey

- Turkey breast fillet (1.5 lb.)

The Marinade

- Salt – ½ teaspoon
- Peanut powder – 1 teaspoon
- Allspice – 1 teaspoon
- Garlic powder – 1 teaspoon
- Onion powder – 1 teaspoon
- Nutmeg – ½ teaspoon
- Sesame oil – ½ teaspoon
- Malt vinegar – 1 cup
- Pineapple juice – ½ cup

The Smoke

- Preheat the smoker at least 15 minutes before grilling.
- Use maple wood pellets for smoking.

METHOD

1. Combine the marinade ingredients in a bowl. Mix thoroughly.
2. Place the turkey breast fillets in the marinade for 18 hours.
3. Remove the breast fillet and dab gently with a paper towel to dry it.
4. Prepare your grill and add maple wood to it. Light it at least 15 minutes before you start grilling.
5. When the grill's temperature reaches 350°F, place the breast fillet on the grate. Grill each side until the internal temperature is 170°F.
6. Remove the breast fillet from the grill. Wrap in foil paper for 20 minutes.
7. Unwrap, cut then serve.

Juicy Breast Steaks

TOTAL COOK TIME 3 HOURS

Ingredients for 4 servings

The Turkey

- 2 turkey breast steaks (0.5 lb.)

The Marinade

- Lemon juice – 1 cup
- Salt – ½ teaspoon
- Garlic powder – 1 teaspoon
- Onion powder – 1 teaspoon
- Cayenne pepper powder – 2 teaspoons
- Curry powder – 1 teaspoon
- Thyme – ¼ teaspoon

The Garnish

- Cucumber – 2 cucumbers, thinly sliced
- Tomato – 2 tomatoes, thinly sliced

The Smoke

- Preheat the smoker at least 20 minutes before smoking.
- Use hickory wood pellets for smoking.

METHOD

1. Combine the ingredients for the marinade in a bowl. Mix thoroughly and set aside.
2. Place the turkey breast steaks in the bowl. Cover the bowl and let the steaks marinate for 12 hours.
3. After marinating, drain the chicken.
4. Prepare your grill, dust it, clean the grates, and remove the ashes. Then add hickory wood to the grill. Light the grill at least 20 minutes before smoking.
5. When the grill reaches 350°F, place the turkey breast steaks on it, and grill each side until the internal temperature is 160°F.
6. Remove the steaks from the grill and allow to stand for 20 minutes.
7. Cut then serve.

Chapter 5/ Fish

Tuna Burgers

TOTAL COOK TIME 45 MINUTES

INGREDIENTS FOR 4SERVINGS

THE FISH

- Tuna steak, ground (2-lbs, 0.9-kgs)

THE INGREDIENTS

- Oil
- 2 medium-size eggs
- Worcestershire sauce – 1 teaspoon
- 1 white onion, diced
- 1 green bell pepper, diced
- Blackened seasoning - 1 tablespoon
- Salmon seasoning – 1 tablespoon

THE SMOKE

- When you are ready to cook; with the lid closed, preheat your grill to smoke and establish the fire for 4-5 minutes.
- Mesquite pellets are recommended for this recipe

METHOD

1. In a bowl, combine the tuna with the eggs, Worcestershire sauce, onion, bell pepper, blackened seasoning and salmon seasoning.
2. Lightly oil clean hands and form the mixture into patties. Avoid over-handling the mixture.
3. Arrange the patties on the hottest part of the grill and cook for between 10-15 minutes, flipping them over halfway through grill time.

Savory Smoked Sardine

TOTAL COOK TIME 35 MINUTES

Ingredients for 6 servings

The Fish

- 6 whole sardines

The Marinade

- Salt – 1 ½ teaspoon
- Honey – 1 tablespoon
- Garlic powder – 2 teaspoons
- Onion powder – 1 teaspoon
- Oregano – ½ teaspoon
- Nutmeg – ½ teaspoon
- Peanut oil – 1 tablespoon
- Apple cider vinegar – 1 ½ cup

The Garnish

- Shredded cabbage – 1 cup
- Beetroots – 3, thinly sliced

The Smoke

- Preheat the smoker at least 15 – 20 minutes before grilling.
- Use oak wood pellets for smoking.

METHOD

1. Combine the marinade ingredients in a bowl. Mix thoroughly.
2. Place the sardines in the marinade for 24 hours.
3. Remove the sardines and drain.
4. Prepare your grill by removing ashes and cleaning the grate.
5. Add oak wood to the grill. Light it at least 15 minutes before you start grilling.
6. Place the sardines on the grate and grill each side at 250°F for 10 minutes.
7. Remove the sardines from the grill and let it stand for 10 minutes.
8. Garnish them with cabbage and beetroots, then serve.

Please Sir, Can I Have Salmon?

TOTAL COOK TIME 35 MINUTES

Ingredients for 4 servings

The Fish

- 4 salmon fillets

The Marinade

- Lemon juice – ½ cup
- Caramel sauce – ½ cup
- Honey – 2 tablespoons
- Salt – ½ teaspoon
- Garlic powder – 1 teaspoon
- Onion powder – 1 teaspoon
- Cayenne pepper powder – 2 teaspoons
- Turmeric powder – 1 teaspoon

The Garnish

- White radish – 2 cucumbers, thinly sliced
- Tomato – 2 tomatoes, thinly sliced

The Smoke

- Preheat the smoker at least 20 minutes before smoking.
- Use mesquite wood pellets for smoking.

METHOD

1. Combine the ingredients for the marinade in a bowl. Mix thoroughly and set aside.
2. Place the salmon fillets in the bowl. Cover the bowl and let them marinate for 10 hours.
3. After marinating, drain the salmon fillets. Dab the fillets gently with a paper towel to dry.
4. Prepare your grill, dust it, clean the grates, and remove the ashes. Then add mesquite wood to the grill. Light the grill at least 20 minutes before smoking.
5. Place the salmon fillets on the grate when the grill is at 400°F. Grill the fillets on each side for 9 minutes.
6. Remove the fillets from the grill and allow to stand for 15 minutes.
7. Garnish them with radishes and tomatoes. Then serve.

SMOKE AT THE BAY

TOTAL COOK TIME 20 MINUTES

INGREDIENTS FOR 4 SERVINGS

THE SEAFOOD

- Wet bay scallop (1 lb.)

The Rub

- Salt – ½ teaspoon
- Garlic powder – 1 teaspoon
- Onion powder – 1 teaspoon
- Cumin – ½ teaspoon
- Nutmeg – ½ teaspoon
- Red pepper flakes – ½ teaspoon

The Smoke

- Preheat the smoker at least 15 minutes before grilling.
- Use heather wood pellets for smoking.

Method

1. Dry the scallops gently with a dry paper towel.
2. Combine the rub ingredients in a bowl. Mix thoroughly.
3. Add the scallops to the bowl containing the rub. Shake the bowl thoroughly to mix.
4. Clean your grill, add heather wood to it, then light it.
5. When the grill is at 450°F, place the seasoned scallops on the grate and grill each side for 4 minutes or until the scallops are opaque.
6. Remove the sardines from the grill and let it stand for 10 minutes.
7. Then serve.

Shrimps on Fire

TOTAL COOK TIME 35 MINUTES

Ingredients for 4 servings

The Seafood

- Deveined shrimps (1 lb.)

THE RUB

- Peanut butter – 2 tablespoons
- Salt – ½ teaspoon
- Garlic powder – 1 teaspoon
- Onion powder – 1 teaspoon
- Cayenne pepper powder – 2 teaspoons
- Paprika – ½ teaspoon
- Cardamom powder – ½ teaspoon

THE SMOKE

- Preheat the smoker at least 20 minutes before smoking.
- Use pecan wood pellets for smoking.

METHOD

1. Combine the rub ingredients in a bowl and mix thoroughly.
2. Add the shrimps to this bowl and stir thoroughly to ensure the shrimps are well covered in the rub. Let the seasoned shrimp sit for 30 minutes.
3. Hold the shrimps together with metal skewers.
4. Prepare your grill. Add heather wood to the grill. Light the grill and allow it to preheat for 20 minutes.
5. Place the shrimps on the grate when the grill is at 350°F. Grill the shrimps on each side for 10 minutes.
6. Remove the shrimps from the grill and allow to stand for 15 minutes.
7. Serve when the shrimps are warm.

Chapter 6/ Vegetables

Smoked Potatoes with Honey

TOTAL COOK TIME 1 HOUR 40 MINUTES

Ingredients for 4 servings

The Vegetable

- Potatoes (1 lb.)

The Rub

- Honey – 4 tablespoons
- Salt – ½ teaspoon
- Onion powder – 1 teaspoon
- Peppercorn powder – 1 teaspoon
- Sage powder – 1 teaspoon
- Cardamom powder – 1 teaspoon

The Second Rub

- Canola oil – 1 tablespoon

The Smoke

- Preheat the smoker at least 15 minutes before smoking.
- Use maple pellets wood for smoking.

METHOD

1. Peel the potatoes and cut into your preferred shapes.
2. Combine the ingredients for the rub in a bowl and mix thoroughly.
3. Add the potatoes to the bowl containing the rub. Stir thoroughly until the rub covers the potatoes very well.
4. Let the potatoes stand for 2 hours.
5. Place the potatoes in heavy-duty foil, wrap until the foils are well sealed.
6. Add maple wood to the grill. Light the grill at least 15 minutes before smoking.
7. Place the foils on the grate when the grill is at 200°F. Grill for 70 minutes.
8. Remove the foils from the grill and allow them to stand for 30 minutes.
9. Serve the potatoes when they are warm.

RAD RADISH

TOTAL COOK TIME 30 MINUTES

Ingredients for 4 Servings

The Vegetable

- Radish (1 lb.)

The Rub

- Salt – ¾ teaspoon
- Onion powder – 1 teaspoon
- Oregano – ½ teaspoon
- Ground black pepper – ½ teaspoon
- Nutmeg – ½ teaspoon
- Peanut oil – 1 tablespoon

The Smoke

- Preheat the smoker at least 15 minutes before grilling.
- Use maple wood pellets for smoking.

METHOD

1. Cut the radishes into thick slices.
2. Combine the rub ingredients in a bowl. Mix thoroughly.
3. Rub the spices mixture on the radishes generously. Let it stand for 40 minutes.
4. Remove the ashes in your grill and clean the grate.
5. Add maple wood to the grill. Light it and preheat for 15 minutes.
6. When the grill reaches 400°F, place the radishes on the grate.
7. Grill each side of the radishes for 9 minutes.
8. Remove the radishes from the grill, wrap them in a layer of foil, and let them stand for 10 minutes.
9. Unwrap and serve when warm.

Smoked Butternut Squash

TOTAL COOK TIME 1 HOURS 35 MINUTES

Ingredients for 4 servings

The Vegetable

- 1 large butternut squash

The Ingredients

- Olive oil – 2 tablespoons
- Sea salt, to season – 2 teaspoons

THE SMOKE

- Preheat your smoker to 275°F
- Cherry wood pellets work well with this recipe

METHOD

1. First prepare the squash by cutting the stem end off approximately 1-ins (2.5-cms) from the very top.
2. Lightly brush the squash with olive oil and season with salt.
3. Arrange the squash on the smoker and cook until softened, for 90 minutes.

Chapter 7 / Game

Rabbit in The Grill Light

TOTAL COOK TIME 1 HOUR

Ingredients for 5 servings

The Game

- Whole skinned rabbit

The Rub

- Salt – 1 teaspoon
- Rosemary powder – 1 teaspoon
- Garlic powder – 1 teaspoon
- Onion powder – 1 teaspoon
- Nutmeg – ½ teaspoon
- Chili powder – ½ teaspoon

The Smoke

- Preheat the smoker at least 15 minutes before grilling.
- Use apple wood for smoking.

Method

1. Combine the rub ingredients in a bowl. Mix thoroughly.
2. Apply the rub all over the rabbit generously. Le the seasoned rabbit sit for 75 minutes.
3. Prepare your grill. Add applewood to the grill and light it for 15 minutes before you grill.
4. Place the rabbit on the grate when the grill is at 400°F. Grill for 20 minutes on each side or until internal temperature is 160°F.
5. Remove the rabbit from the grill and let it stand for 20 minutes.
6. Cut into pieces then serve.

Go and Venison No More

TOTAL COOK TIME 1 HOUR 10 MINUTES

Ingredients for 4 servings

The Game

- 3 inches venison steak (1.5 lb.)

The Marinade

- Peanut oil – ½ cup
- Rice vinegar – ¼ cup
- Soy sauce – 2 tablespoons
- Salt – ¼ teaspoon
- Garlic powder – 1 teaspoon
- Onion powder – 2 teaspoons
- Rosemary powder – 1 teaspoon
- Sage powder – 1 teaspoon

The Smoke

- Preheat the smoker at least 30 minutes before smoking.
- Use hickory wood for smoking.

METHOD

1. Combine the ingredients for the marinade in a bowl. Mix thoroughly and set aside.
2. Place the venison steak in the bowl. Cover the bowl, place the bowl in a fridge, and let it marinate for 14 hours.
3. After marinating, dab the steak gently with a paper towel to dry it.
4. Add hickory wood to the grill. Light the grill at least 30 minutes before smoking.
5. Place the venison steak on the grate when the grill is at 400°F. Grill the steak on each side until the internal temperature is 145°F.
6. Remove the steak from the grill and allow to stand for 30 minutes.
7. Cut into pieces, then serve.

Smoked Duck Legs

TOTAL COOK TIME 5 HOURS 45 MINUTES

Ingredients for 4 servings

The Meat

- 6 duck legs

THE MARINADE

- Kosher salt – ¼ cup
- 4 garlic cloves, peeled, ground to a paste
- Shallot, chopped – ¼ cup
- Zest of 1 orange
- Thyme, chopped – 1 tablespoon
- 1 bay leaf, crushed
- Zest of 1 lemon

THE POLENTA

- Chicken stock – 5 cups
- Coarsely ground polenta – 1 cup
- Kosher salt
- Unsalted butter – 2 tablespoons

THE MUSHROOMS

- Unsalted butter – 2 tablespoons
- Wild mushrooms, sliced – 3 cups
- Chicken stock – ½ cup
- Salt and black pepper
- Fresh thyme leaves – ½ tablespoon

THE SMOKE

- When you are ready to cook, with the lid open, and the grill on smoke establish the fire, for 4-5 minutes.
- Set the temperature to 180°F and with the lid closed

METHOD

1. In a mixing bowl, combine the salt with the garlic paste, shallot, thyme, bay leaf, lemon zest and orange zest.
2. Cover the duck legs with the salt-zest mixture and transfer to the fridge, overnight.
3. Remove the duck legs from the mixture and thoroughly rinse before patting dry.
4. Arrange the duck legs directly on the grate and smoke until the duck shreds easily off the bone, for 4-5 hours.
5. To prepare the polenta, bring the stock to boil in a pan over moderate high heat.
6. Once the stock comes to boil, add the polenta while whisking to eliminate any lumps.
7. Turn down to simmer and cook until the polenta is al dente. You can add a drop more stock if the grain appears too dry. Season with salt and stir in the butter. Keep the polenta warm.
8. To cook the mushrooms: Over high heat, in a pan melt the butter.
9. Add the mushrooms and cook until slightly crispy and gently browned.
10. Add the chicken stock, salt and pepper and transfer to the grill set at a temperature of 350°F and cook for between 20-30 minutes, while the legs are resting.
11. Garnish with thyme and

CONCLUSION

I am happy and proud to have been able to offer you this wood pellet recipe cookbook and I am extremely happy that I have introduced you to the world of wood pellet grills and I am excited to hear your suggestions and how the cooking results will be. This cookbook would have never come to life without your help and support.

Please, feel free to share your thoughts with us and to help us create the healthy environment you want. Get ready to enjoy some of the most entertaining cooking experiences that you will ever be able to enjoy.

WOOD PELLET
SMOKER
COOKBOOK
The Best Recipes Included to Smoke and Grill Meat, Fish, Game, and Etc.
CHAD DAVIS

LEGAL NOTICE

DISCLAIMER NOTICE

WOOD PELLET
SMOKER
COOKBOOK
The Best Recipes Included to Smoke and
Grill Meat, Fish, Game, and Etc.
CHAD DAVIS

Printed in Great Britain
by Amazon

51344922R00052